GETTING TO KNOW THE WORLD'S GREATEST ARTISTS

R E N É
MAGRITTE

WRITTEN AND ILLUSTRATED BY MIKE VENEZIA

CHILDREN'S PRESS®
A DIVISION OF SCHOLASTIC INC.
NEW YORK TORONTO LONDON AUCKLAND SYDNEY
MEXICO CITY NEW DELHI HONG KONG
DANBURY, CONNECTICUT

Cover: *The Son of Man,* by René Magritte. 1964, lithograph, 116 x 89 cm.
© Art Resource, NY/Private Collection/Giraudon. © 2002 C. Herscovici, Brussels/Artists Rights Society
(ARS), New York.

Colorist for illustrations: Dave Ludwig

Library of Congress Cataloging-in-Publication Data

Venezia, Mike.
  René Magritte / written and illustrated by Mike Venezia.
    p. cm. — (Getting to know the world's greatest artists)
Summary: Describes the life and career of the twentieth-century Belgian
Surrealist painter.
  ISBN 0-516-22029-2 (lib. bdg.)   0-516-27814-2 (pbk.)
  1. Magritte, René, 1898-1967—Juvenile literature. 2.
Painters—Belgium—Biography—Juvenile literature. 3.
Surrealism—Juvenile literature. [1. Magritte, René, 1898-1967. 2.
Artists.] I. Magritte, René, 1898-1967. II. Title.
  ND673.M35 V46 2002
  759.9493—dc21

                              2002001608

CHILDREN'S PRESS and associated logos are trademarks
and or registered trademarks of Grolier Publishing Co., Inc.
SCHOLASTIC and associated logos are trademarks and or
registered trademarks of Scholastic Inc.

1 2 3 4 5 6 7 8 9 10 R 11 10 09 08 07 06 05 04 03 02

La Clairvoyance (Percipacity), by René Magritte. 1936, oil on canvas, 54 x 65 cm. © Art Resource, NY/Private Collection. © 2002 C. Herscovici, Brussels/Artists Rights Society (ARS), New York.

René Magritte was born in Lessines, Belgium, in 1898. He became one of the most important members in a group of artists known as the Surrealists. Magritte created strange combinations of objects in his paintings that sometimes seemed funny, surprising, or even frightening.

René Magritte wanted you to think about his paintings and enter a mysterious, magical world. He thought up lots of ways to do this.

Sometimes he put familiar objects in unexpected places. He might combine two objects to make up a third, new, weird one.

The Red Model, by René Magritte. 1935, oil on canvas laid down on panel, 60 x 45 cm. © Bridgeman Art Library International Ltd., London, New York/Musee National d'Art Moderne, Paris, France, Peter Willi. © 2002 C. Herscovici, Brussels/Artists Rights Society (ARS), New York.

Sometimes Magritte would make something much bigger than it was in real life. He even combined daytime and nighttime in the same scene.

L'Empire des Lumieres (The Dominion of Lights), by René Magritte. 1954, oil on canvas, 146 x 114 cm.
© Art Resource, NY/Musees Royaux des Beaux-Arts, Brussels, Belgium. © 2002 C. Herscovici,
Brussels/Artists Rights Society (ARS), New York.

René Magritte lived in Lessines with his parents and two younger brothers. As an adult, he hardly ever talked about his childhood, except for two or three things that really stuck in his mind. One event happened early one morning when he was a little boy. A hot-air balloon crashed onto the roof of the Magrittes' house. The only way the balloonists could get it down was to bring it in through a window and carry it down the stairway. René woke up just in time to see the remarkable event. He never forgot that surprising, unexpected scene.

Another important event happened when Magritte was six or seven years old. Whenever he visited his grandmother, René and a little neighbor girl would sneak into and explore a nearby abandoned cemetery. The cemetery was mysterious and scary.

One day, while coming up the stairs of a dark burial vault, Magritte saw an artist painting a scene of the cemetery. René thought this was the most amazing thing he had ever seen. To him, the artist seemed to have magical powers. It was right there on the spot that René Magritte decided he would become an artist too.

When Magritte was fourteen years old, a terrible thing happened. For some unexplained reason, his mother took her own life. Soon after this, Mr. Magritte decided to move his family away from Lessines and the sad memories there. In 1912, the Magrittes moved to Charleroi, another city in Belgium.

In Charleroi, René took art lessons and spent a lot of time reading mystery books. He loved going to the movies with his brother, Paul. Their favorite movie series was about the mysterious character Fantômas.

Fantômas was an unusual hero because he was a criminal and did disgraceful things. Even so, he became a very popular character. Later, Magritte would paint pictures of this mysterious hero.

Le Retour de Flamme (Backfire), by René Magritte. 1943, oil on canvas, 65 x 50 cm. © Art Resource, NY.
© 2002 C. Herscovici, Brussels/ADAGP/Artists Rights Society (ARS), New York.

The Studio, by Alfred Stevens. oil on canvas, 94 x 71 cm.
© Superstock, Inc./Musees Royaux des Beaux-Arts,
Brussels/AKG, Berlin.

When Magritte was
eighteen years old, he
decided to go to the Royal
Academy of Fine Arts,
a famous art school
in Brussels. Brussels
was the capital city of
Belgium. Magritte's life
had been filled with
unusual, shocking, and
remarkable events. That
may have been part of the
reason why he found the
Academy
and all the
art he saw
in Brussels
pretty boring.

*Sailing Vessels & a Steamship
Offshore in a Squall,* by Louis
Verboeckhoven. oil on canvas.
© Superstock, Inc.

Magritte thought that none of the popular paintings of the day or the past were even worth looking at!

Three Musicians, by Pablo Picasso. 1921, oil on canvas, 204.5 x 188.3 cm. © Philadelphia Museum of Art, A.E. Gallatin Collection, photo by Graydon Wood. © 2002 Estate of Pablo Picasso/Artists Rights Society (ARS), New York.

It was at this time that René Magritte decided to find a new way of painting—a way that would matter to *him*. While searching for a new way to paint, Magritte discovered the latest work being done by Spanish artist Pablo Picasso and German artist Max Ernst. Magritte liked these artists' new, exciting, works. He thought that following their styles might lead him to a new way of painting.

Two Children are Threatened by a Nightingale, by Max Ernst. 1924, oil on wood with wood construction, 69.8x57.1x11.4 cm. © Museum of Modern Art, New York/ Purchase. © 2002 Artists Rights Society (ARS), New York/ADAGP, Paris.

Georgette au Piano (Georgette at the Piano), by René Magritte. 1921, oil on canvas, 43.1 x 36 cm.
© Art Resource, NY. © 2002 C. Herscovici, Brussels/ADAGP/Artists Rights Society (ARS), New York.

The painting above by Magritte reminds many people of Picasso's Cubism period.

The Song of Love,
by Giorgio de Chirico.
1914, oil on canvas,
73 x 59.1 cm. © Museum
of Modern Art, New York,
Nelson A. Rockefeller
Bequest. © 2002 Artists
Rights Society (ARS),
New York/SIAE, Rome.

René Magritte soon realized that in order
to satisfy himself, he would have to make
paintings that did more than just follow
someone else's style. Finally, he came up with
a very exciting idea. What Magritte wanted
to do with his artwork was to show *thought!*

Now he just had to figure out how to do it. Luckily, one day a friend showed Magritte a picture of a painting by Italian artist Giorgio de Chirico. Magritte couldn't believe his eyes! This painting was so beautiful and mysterious that he began to cry when he saw it.

Giorgio de Chirico's painting gave Magritte just the inspiration he needed to begin creating his new paintings.

La Fenetre (The Window), by René Magritte. 1925, oil on canvas, 65 x 50 cm. © Art Resource, NY. © 2002 C. Herscovici, Brussels/ADAGP/ Artists Rights Society (ARS), New York.

Le Jockey Perdu (The Lost Jockey), by René Magritte. 1926, oil on canvas, 65 x 75 cm.© Art Resource, NY/Private Collection/Giraudon. © 2002 C. Herscovici, Brussels/Artists Rights Society (ARS), New York.

The Window and *The Lost Jockey* are two of the first paintings in which Margritte rearranged familiar objects in a new, mysterious way.

The Discovery of Fire, by René Magritte. 1930, oil on canvas, 35.5 x 40.5 cm. © Bridgeman Art Library International Ltd., London, New York/Private Collection. © 2002 C. Herscovici, Brussels/Artists Rights Society (ARS), New York.

René Magritte usually made his paintings a little difficult to understand. He did this on purpose because he wanted people to think about the mysteries of his pictures.

La Condition Humane (The Human Condition), by René Magritte. 1933, oil on canvas, 100 x 81 cm. © Art Resource, NY/Private Collection/ Giraudon. © 2002 C. Herscovici, Brussels/ Artists Rights Society (ARS), New York.

Magritte often gave his paintings titles that made understanding them even more confusing.

Georgette, by René Magritte. 1935, oil on canvas, 65 x 75.5 cm. © Christie's Images.
© 2002 C. Herscovici, Brussels/Artists Rights Society (ARS), New York.

By the time he started doing his new paintings, Magritte had fallen in love with and married a girl he had met in his hometown years before. Her name was Georgette. Georgette was very interested in art too. She worked in an art-supply store, which came in very handy.

Tonny's Toffee Antoine poster, by René Magritte. 1931, color lithograph, 26.7 x 45.4 cm.
© Art Resource, NY. © 2002 C. Herscovici, Brussels/Artists Rights Society (ARS), New York.

Georgette could get her husband paints and brushes at a discounted price. Magritte wasn't selling many of his paintings at this time. He and Georgette were fairly poor. To make extra money, Magritte took a job designing wallpaper in a wallpaper factory. He sometimes made advertising posters too.

Architectonic Angelus of Millet, by Salvador Dali. 1933,
oil on canvas, 73 x 60 cm. © Art Resource, NY/Perls Gallery,
NY/Giraudon. © 2002 Salvador Dali, Gala-Salvador Dali
Foundation/Artists Rights Society (ARS), New York.

Mama, Papa is Wounded! by Yves Tanguy. 1927, oil on
canvas, 92.1 x 73 cm. © Museum of Modern Art, New York,
Purchase. © 2002 Estate of Yves Tanguy/Artists Rights
Society (ARS), New York.

In 1927, René and Georgette moved from
Brussels to Paris, France, to join the Surrealist
artists there. Surrealist painters such as
Salvador Dali and Yves Tanguy believed that
artists could make important and imaginative
art by painting images from dreams and
thoughts that popped into their minds.
Magritte had similar ideas, but he didn't get
along that well with the group.

First of all, he thought the behavior of these artists was too showy and odd. Magritte also preferred to spend a lot of time thinking about the images he painted before he put them into a painting. Finally, the Surrealist leader, Andre Bretón, treated René and Georgette rudely one night. After spending three years in Paris, the Magrittes happily moved back to Brussels.

Golconde, by René Magritte. 1953, oil on canvas, 80.7 x 100.6 cm. © Art Resource, NY/Menil Collection, Houston, TX/Giraudon. © 2002 C. Herscovici, Brussels/Artists Rights Society (ARS), New York.

Even though he didn't have a great experience in Paris, René Magritte discovered a lot about painting from the Surrealists' ideas. Now back home in Brussels, he and Georgette could lead a quiet, normal life. René Magritte didn't need a lot of excitement in his life to be happy.

Le Cicerone, by René Magritte. 1947, oil on canvas, 54 x 65 cm. © Art Resource, NY/Private Collection.
© 2002 C. Herscovici, Brussels/ADAGP/Artists Rights Society (ARS), New York.

He never wanted an art studio and preferred to paint in his dining room. He usually wore a suit while he worked, and sometimes his favorite bowler hat. René Magritte began to create his most famous works now.

René Magritte was always interested in putting images together that were surprisingly different, but at the same time had something in common. In *Elective Affinities,* for instance, the egg and the cage are different objects—but they are both made to hold a bird.

Magritte also liked to point out that painted images are not the same as the real object. In the picture below, the French words say "This is not a pipe." At first, you might think, "what do you mean—that *is* a pipe!" But after thinking about it, you would realize it's not what it first seems to be. Magritte's pipe can't be picked up and smoked. It's only paint on canvas.

La Trahison des Images: "Ceci n'est pas une pipe" (The Betrayal of Images: "This is not a pipe"),
by René Magritte. 1929, oil on canvas, 60 x 81 cm. © Bridgeman Art Library International Ltd. London, New York/Los Angeles County Museum of Art, CA. © 2002 C. Herscovici, Brussels/Artists Rights Society (ARS), New York.

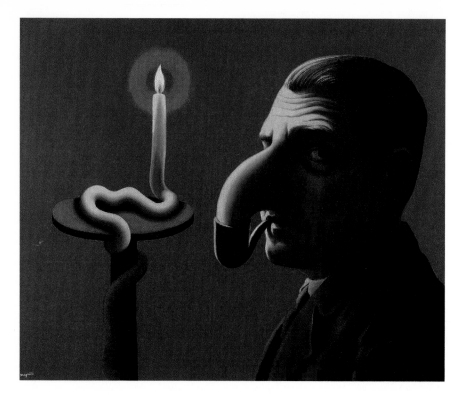

La Lampe Philosophique (The Lamp of Philosophy), by René Magritte. 1936, oil on canvas, 46 x 55 cm. © Art Resource, NY/Private Collection. © 2002 C. Herscovici, Brussels/ ADAGP/ Artists Rights Society (ARS), New York.

René Magritte died in 1967 at the age of sixty-eight. He wanted his paintings to have the power to surprise and delight you. He called this power "poetry." Magritte always looked for ways of painting images that were the opposite of what people expected to see. His paintings are some of the most original and popular of the twentieth century.

Works of art in this book can be seen at the following places:

Art Institute of Chicago
Los Angeles County Museum of Art
Menil Collection, Houston
Musee National d'Art Moderne, Paris
Musées Royaux des Beaux-Arts, Brussels
Museum of Modern Art, New York
Philadelphia Museum of Art